Rudolf Steiner's Re

By the same author

The Cycle of the Year as a Path of Initiation Leading to an Experience of the Christ Being
The East in the Light of the West, Part 1: Agni Yoga
Eternal Individuality, Towards a Karmic Biography of Novalis
The Occult Significance of Forgiveness
Prophecy of the Russian Epic
Rudolf Steiner and the Founding of the New Mysteries
The Spiritual Origins of Eastern Europe and the Future Mysteries of the Holy Grail
The Twelve Holy Nights and the Spiritual Hierarchies

Rudolf Steiner's Research into Karma and the Mission of the Anthroposophical Society

Sergei O. Prokofieff

TEMPLE LODGE
London

Translated by Richard Michell

Temple Lodge Publishing
51 Queen Caroline Street
London W6 9QL

Published by Temple Lodge 1995

Originally published in German under the title *Die Karma-Forschung Rudolf Steiners und die Aufgaben der Anthroposophischen Gesellschaft* by Verlag am Goetheanum, Dornach, in 1994

© Verlag am Goetheanum 1994
This translation © Temple Lodge Publishing 1995

The moral right of the author has been asserted under the Copyright, Designs and Patents Act, 1988

All rights reserved. No part of this publication may be reproduced, stored in a retrieval system, or transmitted, in any form or by any means, electronic, mechanical, photocopying, recording or otherwise, without the prior permission of the publishers.

A catalogue record for this book is available from the British Library

ISBN 0 904693 69 4

Cover: art by Fergus Anderson, design by S. Gulbekian
Typeset by DP Photosetting, Aylesbury, Bucks
Printed and bound in Great Britain by Cromwell Press Limited, Broughton Gifford, Wiltshire

Preface

I have reworked the contents of a lecture into the present written form at the instigation of Frédéric Kozlik (who died on 22 September 1989), the founder and director of the 'Paul of Tarsus' branch of the Anthroposophical Society in Alsace.

The lecture was originally given in German on 15 October 1988 during the conference organized by Frédéric Kozlik at Mont Ste Odile (Odilienberg) and was rendered simultaneously by him into French.

May this small publication also bear witness to this individuality who was so deeply dedicated to Anthroposophy. His fruitful work in the fields of Anthroposophy, teaching and publishing, as well as his own unusual destiny, made him a natural mediator between the Slavonic East, Middle Europe and his native France.

Sergei O. Prokofieff
Stuttgart, Easter 1994

In looking at the cultural history of the West, and in particular at the idea of reincarnation and karma, we can become aware that two individualities have played a decisive but in a certain sense an opposing role in its development. The idea of reincarnation can still be found in Plato, for example, especially in his later works such as *The Republic*.[1] But his treatment of the concept has a strong oriental colouring, so that at times we cannot easily distinguish it from the teaching of metempsychosis, the transmigration of souls. Yet the idea was taken for granted by Plato and by many philosophers and mystery schools in earlier times. The other individuality was responsible for eliminating the notion of reincarnation from western culture—in whose earlier periods it is certainly to be found—so that the consciousness of western man was concentrated on a single Earth life. This great change wrought by Aristotle has been of world-historical importance in the development of the western mind. Aristotle was a pupil of Plato for almost 18 years. Later, after he had founded his own school and developed his own teaching, he turned away totally from the idea of reincarnation.[2] Indeed, he went further, and even rejected the idea of the pre-existence of the soul. In so doing, he set western culture along an entirely new path.

The attention of western humanity was directed principally to a *single* life, this unique Earth life into which the lofty divine Being of Christ was to enter 300 years later.

For this reason among others, Aristotle was known in the Middle Ages as the forerunner of Christ in the things of nature (*praecursor Christi in naturabilis*). In time, Aristotle's work became widely disseminated in Europe, and with it his teaching of the uniqueness of a human Earth life. This created the basis for the entire development of the European mind in the Middle Ages, and made the problem of the acceptance or non-acceptance of the Christ-impulse into a problem of the life or death of the soul. A single life had to acquire this pre-eminent importance and this immeasurable value—an important precondition for the ego development of western humanity. Thus it can be said that the deed that Aristotle performed with regard to the idea of reincarnation carried humanity over from the sphere of eternal ideas, in which Plato still dwelt, into earthly life, into that life in which alone humanity can encounter the Christ Being.

In the course of many centuries, the human ego gradually gained strength and independence precisely because it had to develop within a single Earth life. As a result, a new step became possible for humanity in our time, at the end of the age of darkness known as Kali Yuga. It is a step in the reverse direction, in which the ego transcends its limited terrestrial existence and achieves a new and fully conscious relationship to the spiritual cosmos, its true spiritual home in which it sojourns between earthly incarnations.

This new step in the development of humanity also had to be initiated by a specific individuality, and this was Rudolf Steiner. He created the basis for the human ego, now grown strong, to extend its gaze, its horizon, beyond the boundary of this one life and enter into a new and conscious relationship to the spiritual cosmos. He restored the idea of reincarnation and karma to humanity but in a new and now wholly Christian form. As a result, every human being can now experience himself differently within the course of world development. A pathway was opened for human beings to experience their higher ego that is connected with the entire cosmos.

Rudolf Steiner often stressed that the laws of karma are among the highest laws of the cosmos and permeate our entire visible and invisible world. They are so comprehensive that they work through all the Hierarchies weaving their deeds in the cosmos, and link the highest spiritual sphere directly with the physical world. So if we are to understand these forces of karma, we must inevitably enter into relationship with the highest spirituality of the world. For these karmic laws reveal the activity of the exalted First Hierarchy, which represents the highest Father-force in our world and allows it to flow into that world. So to understand the laws of karma means to come into contact with the Father-ground of the universe, the primeval foundation that simultaneously encompasses the spiritual and physical worlds.

Thus research into the sphere of karma penetrates into the very being and activity of the powers of karma and forms the basis of the modern spiritual science of

Anthroposophy. For only by learning to understand these laws can the human being realize how spiritual forces work simultaneously in man and the cosmos and link the two into a higher unity.

Rudolf Steiner was intimately concerned with the subject of karma from a very early stage. In *The Course of My Life*, he describes how he had his first experiences in this field when he was around 27 or 28. And he gathered further experience of this kind while working on his book *The Philosophy of Freedom*. Later, when he began to teach what was to become Anthroposophy openly at the beginning of this century, he wanted to introduce the subject from the very start in the form of practical karmic exercises. The teaching about the Hierarchies, which was to form a basic element of Anthroposophy, is also inseparable from an understanding of the way that the laws of karma work in the world. For *all* the Hierarchies work in various ways in the shaping of world karma.[3] And the evolution of the world researched by Rudolf Steiner, which goes back to the Old Saturn period, is intimately linked to the effects of karma. This is because the cosmic laws underlying the creation by the First Hierarchy of the cosmos of Old Saturn and the associated first elements of the human physical body work today as the laws of individual karma.[4] In various guises and in different ways, this subject can be found like a red thread running through Rudolf Steiner's entire corpus of lectures, to find its full culmination in the 83 lectures on karma that he gave at the end of his life in 1924.

However, this connection between the laws of karma and the highest and most profound spirituality of the world means that a human being cannot attempt to perform direct research into karma without undergoing an extensive transformation of his own being. We can observe this in Rudolf Steiner's own work as a teacher of the spirit. The suggestions that he gave his various pupils in different situations were always associated with research into karma. But Rudolf Steiner could pursue this research only because he connected his own karma with that of his pupil in every single case. And he indicated this necessity, which must always be respected when performing research into karma, in his Mystery Plays. Thus Benedictus says:

> I must accompany each one who has received
> from me the spirit-light in earthly existence,
> whether he came to me as a pupil of the spirit
> knowingly, or did so without awareness;
> and I must guide him further along the path
> that he has begun to tread in the spirit
> by virtue of my deed.[5]

The Christmas Conference is a momentous example of how a teacher links his being with the pupils that he must guide for karmic reasons. It was then that Rudolf Steiner linked himself to the karma of the Society[6] and then told the assembled anthroposophists something of his own karma and that of the Society,[7] so that he might also reveal their own karma to them. Behind this deed stands a real spiritual process. For in our time, when the Christ is increasingly becoming the Lord of Karma,[8] no one can enter the sphere of karma without becoming a follower of Christ, without practising *imitatio Christi*, and thus assuming the karma of others in some way or other. Rudolf Steiner once described this process in connection with an early Christian community in his lecture cycle on the Gospel of St Matthew: 'A single member of the community commits a wrongful deed. It will certainly be inscribed in the karma of the person concerned, and must be worked out in macrocosmic relationships. But another person may come who says: "I will help you bear your karma!" The karma must be fulfilled, but someone else can help the perpetrator. Thus entire communities can help someone who has done an evil deed. The individual can entwine his own karma with the community so that—because the community regards him as one of its members—he is relieved in full awareness of something that concerns him. The entire community then feels and wills as one to improve the individual, so that it can say: "You as an individual have done wrong, but we shall intercede for you! We will take upon ourselves whatever shall bring about correction of your karma."'[9]

In this context, there is naturally every justification to provide information about a specific case of reincarnation of a real person. But if we really study Rudolf Steiner's lectures on karma, we note that this was never his sole aim. Neither were such specific details revealed by Anthroposophy alone. Thus we can find concrete indications about the former incarnations of Pythagoras in a biography written by the Neoplatonist philosopher Porphyry.

But what absolutely new element did Rudolf Steiner bring into the world through his research into karma? It was the revelation of the world-encompassing nature of karmic laws in the cosmos and in human life. Rudolf Steiner laid very special stress on the fact that human beings must learn to understand these laws, and must plan and guide their lives and their deeds—and in the future even their entire social structure—from this understanding. For today a knowledge of these laws has the effect of changing a person's relationship to the world and to his own life, allowing him to feel part of the entire cosmos.

The specific examples that Rudolf Steiner described did not merely represent knowledge *per se* to him, but were intended to serve as concrete illustrations of these great laws of karma.

In this sense, the law that Rudolf Steiner formulated in the following way belongs to every true occult development: 'It is an important principle in occult development to assign to oneself only that value which comes from one's achievements in the physical world within the present incarnation.'

In a certain sense, questions born of curiosity such as 'Who was I?' or 'Who was he?' represent the absolute contradiction of this principle. The same applies when anyone tries to obtain knowledge of their previous Earth lives by various external means, by intellectual speculations, by a comparison of horoscopes or by nebulous mystical experiences. Unless this process leads to a fundamental transformation of the human being, giving him a full experience of the cosmos in which he is embedded, such knowledge has no particular value even if it is not false. In the fourth Mystery Play, Ahriman has the following to say about such pseudo-occultists:

> And [the soul] will then appear as an occultist, and when called upon will tell human beings of their lives from the primeval beginnings of the Earth.[10]

The Mystery Plays also tell us that in future human beings will be found who will even practise a kind of research into karma. But these people will be inspired by ahrimanic powers whose aim is to give them knowledge that does not transform their very nature. They merely receive it passively while remaining exactly as they were. Such knowledge will in the future lead only to the decadence of humanity. A true knowledge of karma stands in complete contrast to this approach. It leads to a religious outlook on the world, because a true knowledge of the laws of karma makes the whole of life into a divine service.

In his book *The Spiritual Guidance of Man and Humanity*, Rudolf Steiner spoke about the twofold inspiration at work in our time: one coming from the retarded and another from the progressive Angels who were active in the Egypto-Chaldean epoch. These Angels are again assuming the guidance of humanity in our fifth post-Atlantean epoch and thus send two different types of inspiration into the world.[11] They can be distinguished clearly on the basis of their distinct relationships to the sphere of karma. The egoistic wish to penetrate this sphere out of mere curiosity is today linked with the inspirations of retarded Angels from the Egypto-Chaldean epoch. But the effort to link up with the laws of karma so that they become a true religious basis for life and gradually transform the entire nature of the human being owes its inspiration to the progressive Angels.

It was from these inspirations that Rudolf Steiner developed his teaching of karma. For if we look more closely at his great lectures on karma from the year 1924, we observe that they are built up methodologically so that concrete examples from the sphere of karma are preceded by a description of general laws. In the same way, the spiritual scientist begins his research into karma with an insight into general laws before he is permitted to approach specific cases. This is connected with the fact that in order to obtain concrete results concerning karma he must have developed the ability to experience the entire life of the soul between death and a new birth in a spiritual way. Only when the spiritual scientist is able to attain a conscious experience of the Midnight Hour of existence can the results of his research into karma be reliable and without errors. Rudolf Steiner gives examples of this in his Mystery Plays. Thus his second Mystery Play tells of experiences relating to karma that are not connected with a conscious experience of the Midnight Hour. The result is that Capesius regards the experiences that he had in a condition of incomplete wakefulness as an illusion, and that Maria and Johannes are plunged into uncertainty by Ahriman and Lucifer. In the fourth Mystery Play, the experience of the Midnight Hour becomes a consciously experienced reality only for Maria, and she therefore achieves reliable knowledge of her own karmic past.

We can summarize the entire process in the following way. To understand the laws of karma, we must understand the entire cosmos. And only an understanding of the entire cosmos can give contemporary human beings an understanding of the nature of man and his karma that is in tune with our times.

Let us now observe the importance that a specific result of Rudolf Steiner's research into karma, in the twentieth century, can have for a human life on the basis of a particular example. We may start from what Rudolf Steiner says about the effect of karmic relationships in human life in his lecture of 18 May 1924 in Dornach.[12] This lecture culminates in a description of how from a karmic standpoint all nine Hierarchies come to alternate manifestation during the seven-year periods of a human life. Rudolf Steiner summarizes this description in the following diagram:

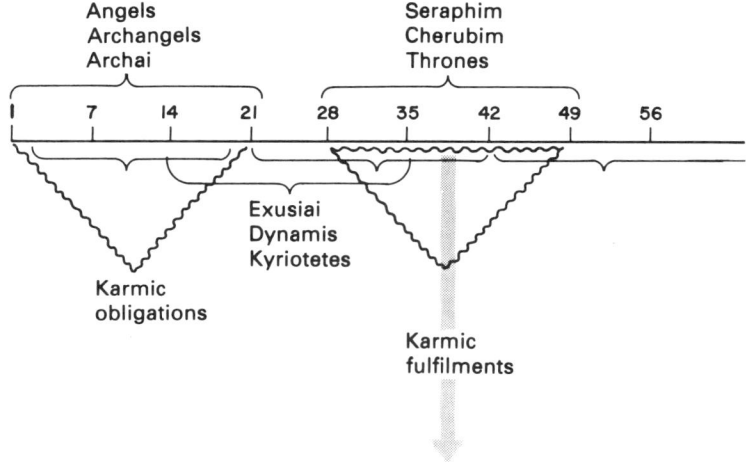

Fig. 1.

In order to understand this relationship somewhat more clearly, we have to include the life of the human being between death and a new birth. During this time, the soul first of all traverses the Moon-sphere and then the Sun-sphere. But any earthly deed that was evil, erroneous or imperfect cannot accompany the human being into the Sun-sphere. He has to leave these behind in the Moon-sphere.[13] However, everything that a human being has ever done in life is linked to his very essence, and if he has to leave his imperfect or evil deeds behind this means that he must leave a part of himself behind. So he enters the higher spiritual world, the Sun-sphere, in an imperfect state, or in a 'stunted' form, as Rudolf Steiner says. And it is in this form that he is perceived in the Sun-sphere by the spiritual beings that are linked with the life of Mars, Jupiter and Saturn. They pass on what they see in the human being to the beings of the Third Hierarchy, the Angels, Archangels and Archai. These beings then impress much of what we lack in this sense in the Sun-sphere into our nerve-sensory system after our birth, so that we can make up for it in our next Earth life. Rudolf Steiner calls this the *karmic obligations* of our coming life. The beings of the Third Hierarchy gradually impress these obligations into us during the first three seven-year periods of our life.

Starting with the fourteenth year, still higher beings enter into human life. From this time onwards and over the next three seven-year periods, the beings of the Second Hierarchy, the Exusiai, Dynamis and Kyriotetes, also work on the human being. They work all the way into the physical body and among other things bring the forces of sexual maturity to the growing human being. But in the further course of life, from the thirty-fifth year onward, the forces of degeneration become increasingly dominant. And if nothing else were to happen, a human being could hardly continue to live as a physical being beyond his thirty-fifth year. That is the reason why somewhat earlier, at around the twenty-eighth year, the still higher First Hierarchy, the exalted beings of the Seraphim, Cherubim and Thrones, intervene in human life and guide man through another three seven-year periods, between the ages of 28 and 49. They give him the forces from the spiritual cosmos for his further life that counter the forces of degeneration working in his physical organism. Now Rudolf Steiner has the following to say as regards this development. The human being obtains the gifts of the Third Hierarchy and later of the Second Hierarchy in a natural way, without having to do anything himself. But his relationship to the First Hierarchy is quite different. Modern man can enter into this relationship only by his own efforts. This is also linked to the fact that human evolution involves a process of gradual rejuvenation. In the Egypto-Chaldean epoch the human being could still continue to develop by virtue of the pre-natal forces working in him up to his forty-second year, in the Graeco-Roman period only up to his thirty-fifth year and today only up to his twenty-eighth year,[14] so that everything that happens to him after that age depends on his own activity. In this sense, therefore, he can link up with the activity of the First Hierarchy in our time only by his own efforts. To do so, he must resist the forces that strive to draw him downwards away from this relation. In the same lecture, Rudolf Steiner says how immeasurably much depends today on the human being finding this relationship to the First Hierarchy between his twenty-eighth and forty-ninth years. He points out the great task of Waldorf education in this regard, that must give the growing child in early life the soul forces that will enable him successfully to negotiate these transitions in later life. Thus Rudolf Steiner states that the greatest possible degree of permeation of the intellect with moral forces is a necessary condition for establishing the right relationship to the First Hierarchy.

This relationship is so vastly important because it is the only means by which the human being can attain what Rudolf Steiner calls *karmic fulfilment* in the middle of his life. In other words, only then is he able to fulfil the 'karmic obligations' that were impressed into the invisible part of his being by the Third Hierarchy at the beginning of his life. However, these karmic fulfilments also contain a significant part of what we may call the meaning of life for modern man. If this relationship is not consciously nurtured, then the beings of the First Hierarchy will continue to work on the human being but they will do so with declining strength from century to century—so that at some point in the future the physical decadence of humanity will become inevitable. And the immediate effect of this incapacity to form such a relationship is a growing inability to achieve a rightful expression of individual karma, in other words to realize this karmic fulfilment.

If the latter does not happen because the forces of this relationship are too weak, then the beings of the First

Hierarchy speak to the unconscious of the human being about his unfulfilled karma as follows: 'All this will remain with you, because you are unable to fulfil it, because you are unable to reach up to us. It will remain with you, and you must carry it over into your next life; you are unable to compensate it—you lack the necessary strength.'[15] In the next lecture Rudolf Steiner talks about the further life of the human being: 'After the forty-ninth year, it is no longer possible to enter into a direct relationship to the Hierarchies.'[16] How are we to understand these words? Here, Rudolf Steiner points to a great mystery of human life. But he does not return to it in the further course of his lectures.

If we endeavour to resolve this problem today, we find a key in another statement by Rudolf Steiner: 'Whoever could not pray in youth cannot bless in old age.' And the following lines can bring us still closer to a solution:

> Stars once spoke to human beings,
> Their muteness is world destiny;
> Awareness of this muteness
> Can mean suffering for earthly man;
>
> But in the mute silence there matures,
> what human beings say to the stars;
> Awareness of this utterance
> Can bring power to Spirit Man.[17]

In these words we glean something of what may happen to a human being when the Hierarchies cease speaking within him. 'When the spirits cease their speaking, then shall human beings start to speak.' But this means that when a man has found his way to the beings of the First Hierarchy between his twenty-eighth and forty-ninth years he has created the foundation for expressing his karma in this life. So after his forty-ninth year, even starting from his forty-second year, he can look back at the life he has lived and try to give back to the Hierarchies what they gave him from the beginning of his life up to his thirty-fifth year. He can then do something that goes beyond his purely 'karmic obligations' and 'karmic fulfilments' and thus beyond the limits set by his karma in this life. Thus between the forty-second and sixty-third years of his life he can return to the beings of the Second Hierarchy in a new form what he received from them between his fourteenth and thirty-fifth years. And between his fifty-sixth and seventy-seventh years he can return to the Third Hierarchy what he received from it in the first three seven-year periods of his life. The human being can achieve this by means of inner development, by working on himself, and by developing a significant interest in spiritual matters. He can make the spiritual achievements of his earlier life fruitful in a social sense, especially in the three seven-year periods that follow his forty-second year. He can let them flow into whatever goes beyond the boundaries of his own enclosed life in a spiritual and social sense. Everything that the human being does in a spirit of active social creativity at this age then streams upwards from him to the beings of the Second Hierarchy. At the beginning of his life he received from them the possibility of sexual maturity and thus creativity in a physical sense. Now he can bring them the fruits of his free *spiritual* creativity.

After his fifty-sixth year, a human being's spiritual life separates more and more from his physical life. The processes of degeneration begin to dominate in the latter. The consequence is that his soul-spiritual forces become increasingly free from the physiological-physical processes. This gives him the inner possibility in the last phase of his life of becoming very much more independent of his corporeality in his soul, of coming closer to the beings of the Third Hierarchy and thus of feeling his soul and spiritual nature to be guided by them. If it is filled with the spirit, everything that he does in this last period of his life can be received directly by the beings of the Third Hierarchy. In this part of his life, therefore, the human being has the disposition to lead a much more spiritual life that is free of the body, and consequently to approach the spiritual world in a much more direct way. He can then also fulfil his obligations with regard to the Third Hierarchy. The Angels, Archangels and Archai led him into life and guided him through his first three seven-year periods. And now the human being can enter into an ever more conscious relationship to these beings by means of his own efforts in the three seven-year periods that lie between his fifty-sixth and seventy-seventh year. He can return to them what he received from them at the dawn of his life. He can also balance out all the errors and one-sidednesses that he was exposed to in his childhood and youth—in the first three seven-year periods—and replace them by creative spiritual impulses that he has consciously grasped.

By virtue of these processes, therefore, the human being can remain linked to the powerful stream of hierarchical existence in the second half of his life. This stream leads him from the First Hierarchy to the Second Hierarchy and then to the Third Hierarchy, and thus allows him to find his way back to the spiritual world.

We may follow Rudolf Steiner in calling this last creative phase (between the ages of 56 and 77) the period of *free karmic sacrifice* in the same sense that he calls the period between 28 and 49 the period of karmic fulfilments and that from birth to 21 the period of karmic obligations.

Through his free karmic sacrifice, the human being can do more in his life than his personal karma demands of him directly. He can become a servant of the world and thus contribute to the world in the sense of the *imitatio Christi*.

Along this path, the human being approaches ever more closely to the spiritual world from which he once entered into life through birth. For although the beings of the First Hierarchy are the highest and most powerful in the hierarchical world order, their activity, which reaches up to the physical structure of existence, is furthest removed from the individual human consciousness.

The beings of the Third Hierarchy are not as powerful and exalted. But they are much closer to what the human being can grasp with his consciousness. Thus the gradual transition from the First to the Second and then to the Third Hierarchy at the same time means an increasingly intense awareness of the spiritual world. And just as the beings of the Third Hierarchy inscribed our karmic obligations into our nerve-sense system (head system) at

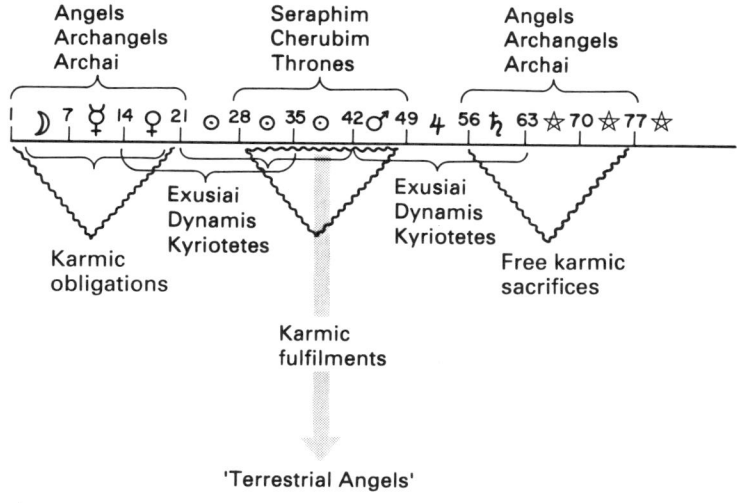

Fig. 2

the beginning of life, they inscribe into it at the end of our life whatever we have freely sacrificed for the development of humanity beyond the obligations of our own karma. That is why there are such wonderful aged visages in the world that bespeak spiritualized experiences and life's wisdom and show how the spirit enters into matter and transforms it. We need think only of the portraits by Rembrandt. This spirituality that manifests as far as the physical expression is carried by such people into the supersensible world after their death. There the etheric formative forces that had shaped their head system are poured into the entire cosmos, becoming the origin of new and future developments. They are taken up especially by those beings that are connected to the spheres of Mars, Jupiter and Saturn.

The tradition has come down to us from ancient times

that a complete human life lasts 72 years. This is also known as the age of patriarchs. It is an important fact that the number 72 lies precisely within the last seven-year period in which free karmic sacrifices are possible. This last period of seven years, which concludes with the age of 77, has quite a special meaning in human life. In earlier lectures, Rudolf Steiner connected the spheres of hierarchical activity with the various planets, namely, Angels with the Moon-sphere, Archangels with the Mercury-sphere, Archai with the Venus-sphere, the Spirits of Form with the Sun, the Spirits of Movement with Mars, the Spirits of Wisdom with Jupiter, the Thrones with Saturn, and the Cherubim and Seraphim with the starry firmament.[18] If we add his comments about how the activity of the planetary forces is linked with the development of the human being in seven-year periods,[19] whereby the three seven-year periods from the twenty-first to the forty-second year are connected to the Sun, then it follows that these hierarchical influences cease at the age of 77 (see Fig. 2).

In the Gospels, too, we find the number 77 in quite a significant connection. Thus at the beginning of St Luke's Gospel, exactly 77 generations are enumerated as coming between Adam as the paradisaical man descended from God and the appearance of Christ at the Turning-point of Time. These 77 stages thus range between the primeval birth of humanity from the bosom of the Godhead and what may be called the overcoming of death at Golgotha. They also link the two Rosicrucian sayings *ex Deo nascimur* and *in Christo morimur*. But it also follows that when a human being maintains his connection with the Hierarchies through his own spiritual activity beyond his forty-ninth year and continues it through to his seventy-seventh year, he can fulfil this second Rosicrucian saying in his own life. For around his seventy-seventh year the human being returns to the starting-point of his life. He now stands in a similar relation to the world of Angels as that which existed at his birth, although in a completely different way. And in our time, this angelic world is under the direct leadership of the Christ.[20] But the human being can continue to live beyond the age of 77. In his inner development, he has then reached the boundary of the hierarchical cosmos and now receives impulses from a still higher, super-hierarchical sphere (beyond the starry firmament). He receives his further Earth life as a pure gift of the spiritual world. He may then already prepare his next Earth life in an inward way and at the same time, with increasing age, make a significant contribution to life on the Earth through his mere physical existence.

But a human being who realizes the *in Christo morimur* in his life will also experience his post-mortal existence in quite a different way. He acquires the opportunity of going through it in a much more conscious way and thus of attaining to the experience of *per spiritum sanctum reviviscimus* after his death.

The connection that he has maintained with the Hierarchies *during his entire life* also gives him something quite different. For his earthly life in the period between birth and the age of 77 then becomes a true mirror image of the life between death and a new birth. In other words, *his earthly life becomes a reflection of his cosmic life and acquires the character of a true divine service.* For after his death the human being dwells first of all in the bosom of the Third Hierarchy, then of the Second, finally reaching the sphere of the First Hierarchy during the Midnight Hour of his post-mortal existence. From this sphere he returns to the Second Hierarchy and is then received by the Third Hierarchy up to his birth. He then lives his earthly life in the same way. After his birth, he links up with the Third Hierarchy, then with the Second and around the middle of his life with the First Hierarchy. And if he has the inner strength to move beyond the boundary of his own life and of his own karmic obligations and fulfilments and to remain in further contact with the Hierarchies by virtue of his free cosmic sacrifice, firstly with the Second and later with the Third Hierarchy, then the path of his earthly life will become a true image of his cosmic existence or of his life between death and a new birth. But the Hierarchies live in the spiritual world in a reverse time stream to that prevailing in the physical world. They move from the future into the past, while we on the Earth move from the past into the future.[21]

If a human being looks back at his life in his later years and reflects upon it from a knowledge of the laws of karma, he brings into his life this spiritualized time stream that flows from the future into the past. He then grows into the spiritual world in a real way. While still dwelling in the physical world, he transforms his life into what may be called a microcosmic image of the great work of art wrought by the Hierarchies in the spiritual cosmos. His life then acquires a higher meaning and deeper religious foundations. It becomes a mirror image on the Earth of the cosmic processes that together represent the cosmic divine service performed by the Hierarchies in the spiritual world and whose influence manifests on the Earth in the form of the all-encompassing laws of karma.

We have already seen how man's entire development in later life depends entirely upon his relationship with the influences of the First Hierarchy at around his twenty-eighth year and thus allows him to express true karmic fulfilments in his life between that age and his forty-ninth year. But the question then arises of how we can find this connection to the First Hierarchy around the

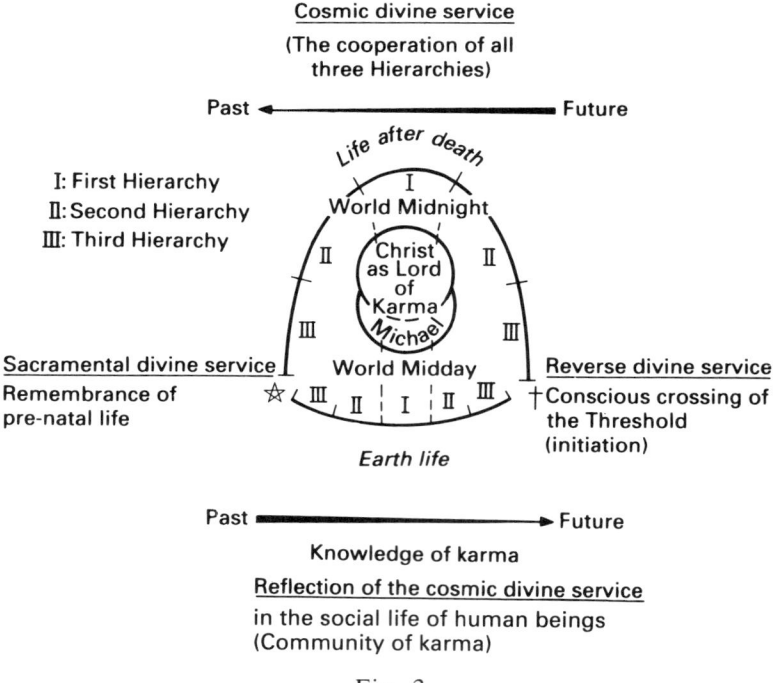

Fig. 3

middle of our lives. Anthroposophy gives an answer to this question. In a lecture of 19 November 1922,[22] Rudolf Steiner describes how every human being in our time has an encounter in the Moon-sphere with the light of Michael and the love substance of the Christ immediately before his birth.

Today, every human being experiences this light and this love before his birth. Michael then shows him the karmic obligations for his coming life in the spiritual light, and through his love Christ awakens in the human soul the ability to accept his own karma, to love it (*amor fati*). This experience is necessary for the human being of today, not only in order to enact his karmic fulfilments after his twenty-eighth year but also to grasp the true impulse of freedom in life. Rudolf Steiner says of this: 'That is the essential point of re-experiencing this post-mortal event in the Moon-sphere [immediately before birth], that there is a moment in cosmic existence where the human being brings his fate, his karma, in line with his own progressive nature in an independent way. And the earthly image of this deed performed in the supersensible realm in the subsequent earthly life is human freedom, the feeling of freedom during Earth life.'[23] And this feeling of freedom forms the basis for the free karmic sacrifices in the second half of life. Human beings usually forget all these experiences after their birth, but it is an important task of Anthroposophy to raise them up into the awareness of modern man. For Anthroposophy is called upon to remind the human being of what he received from Michael and Christ before his birth in order to fulfil his karmic obligations in the coming life.

And because the Christ has now become Lord of Karma, he has also entered into a completely new relationship with the beings of the First Hierarchy who weave karma. The Michael-Christ experience before birth can then find its realization in the time of karmic fulfilments between the twenty-eighth and forty-ninth years of life.

But Rudolf Steiner also spoke of the powers that strive to draw human beings away from this link with the First Hierarchy and from the karmic fulfilments that this involves (see Figs 1 and 2). The beings who wish to do this are Angels who have left the Michael-sphere and are responsible for plunging the karma of modern humanity into disorder.[24]

These Angels have thus become 'terrestrial' Angels who no longer work in the sense of the First Hierarchy in the field of karma, and thus wish to prevent human beings from finding the connection to this Hierarchy in the middle of their lives. In his lectures on karma, Rudolf Steiner drew the attention of the Anthroposophical Society to these great world mysteries. And what did he have to say about the karma of the Anthroposophical Society from our present viewpoint? That this karma is essentially made up of the karmic obligations brought over by the souls of all anthroposophists into their earthly existence. Indeed, they did this from their fraternal togetherness in the supersensible Michael School, from their cooperation in the supersensible divine service,[25] and then as a result of their encounter with Michael-Christ in pre-natal existence, when Michael acted as the Lord of Karma in his capacity as the executive power of Christ. 'But how can those powers arise who cause human beings to come together under purely spiritual principles that are otherwise totally unknown in today's world? What is the nature of these powers that draw men together? They come about through the dominion of Michael, through the age of Michael in which we are living, with the coming of Michael to rulership over the Earth ... Michael brings the power that will again restore order in the karma of those who are his companions. So that we can say: What brings the members of the Anthroposophical Society together? They come together because they want to restore order to their karma!'[26]

Rudolf Steiner had read these karmic obligations spiritually from the souls of the assembled anthroposophists and revealed them in his lectures on karma. And in the preceding Christmas Conference he also created the basis for these karmic obligations to become karmic fulfilments. From our relationship to and intimate concern with the Christmas Conference we can obtain the forces to transform the karmic obligations that we as anthroposophists have brought with us from our prenatal life into karmic fulfilments in this life. We will then be capable of free karmic sacrifice during the last third of our lives, that is, of pursuing the same path taken by Rudolf Steiner himself. But as pupils we must first of all traverse the stages of this path in reverse order from that of the master. When he stood in the age of free karmic sacrifice, Rudolf Steiner performed the great sacrifice of associating his own karma with the Anthroposophical Society in full freedom in order to institute the Christmas Conference and to found the General Anthroposophical Society.

Thus in connection with the Christmas Conference we can observe the following sequence in Rudolf Steiner's life: first of all the free karmic sacrifice involving the risk of a withdrawal by the Michaelic forces that had hitherto been guiding him; then, starting with the Christmas Conference and in an increasing measure afterwards, the karmic fulfilment, the acceptance of his sacrifice by the spiritual powers inspiring the anthroposophical movement;[27] and finally the spiritual obligations for all pupils of Michael on the Earth. These are described in the lectures on the karma of the Anthroposophical Society and especially in the conditions and contents of the First Class. (This refers above all to the supersensible Michael School with its supersensible divine service, whose consequences all anthroposophists bear in their souls as karmic obligations.)

Thus, above all through his lectures on karma, Rudolf Steiner brought these karmic obligations that he had read from their souls to the awareness of anthroposophists and so created the conditions allowing them to fulfil their karma. This will consist in the foundation of the new community permeated by a fraternal spirit and formed by active efforts to restore karmic order within the Society. This will allow the highest Midnight Forces to begin to work as spiritual Midday forces in the social sphere.

In turn, this will create the conditions for finding the way from karmic obligations to a free karmic sacrifice, in other words from the present into the future, to deeds that are free of old karma and can therefore serve as a direct expression of the will of Michael on the *Earth*.

But we must add another aspect that follows from

Rudolf Steiner's research into karma understood in this way. In the lecture of 25 December 1918,[28] Rudolf Steiner brought the course of human life into connection with the three great principles of equality, liberty and fraternity in the following way. The beginning of life stands under the sign of equality, for at this point all human beings on Earth have karmic obligations inscribed into their souls by the beings of the Third Hierarchy. All human beings are equal in this respect, although they may differ greatly otherwise. At the end of life, when the human being learns to become increasingly free from his physical organism in his soul and spirit, he increasingly experiences the true nature of freedom, the freedom in the spirit that finds its culmination at the moment of death.

True freedom lies especially in the moral sphere. For the human being can be freely creative only when this activity results in something new in the world, something not subject to whatever had been previously created. But this means that a human being who has fully expressed the karmic basis of his life in the sense of karmic fulfilments between the ages of 28 and 49 becomes free in his further life in whatever he can now offer to the Hierarchies. He becomes free of old karma, which is always linked to necessities from the past. And this is what will make of humanity the Fourth (Tenth) Hierarchy that will conclude our cosmos in the future, the Hierarchy that will bring into the spiritual cosmos something that did not previously exist in this form. Rudolf Steiner calls it *freedom and love*,[29] free creative activity in the moral sphere originating from pure love. In order to take the first steps in this direction in the last third of his life, however, as we have said, the human being must previously have expressed and balanced out his past karma to a certain degree. For it is precisely past, unredeemed karma that presents the great obstacle to becoming a free moral being.

But what do we need in order to fulfil our karma in the middle of life, especially between the ages of 28 and 49, so that we can be freely creative at the end of our lives? We need something that Rudolf Steiner links specifically to the middle of life, and that is the impulse of *universal brotherhood*. Today, this impulse to brotherhood is linked inseparably with the process of karmic fulfilments, and Michael-Christ calls upon us from our pre-natal existence to realize this impulse. Thus all human beings, and especially anthroposophists, who can consciously recognize the laws of karma thanks to spiritual science, face the great task of using this impulse to create the karmic community of the future. A start must be made in our time by using the forces of Michael-Christ to restore order in karma. The life of human beings on Earth can then increasingly become an image of man's cosmic existence between death and a new birth and can thus acquire a sacramental-ritual character. 'Thus a web is spun by virtue of the threads of the individual being interwoven with the karma of the whole Society. And thanks to what the Christ has brought down from spiritual heights, this web will reflect the order in the heavens. In other words, *the karma of the individual will be linked to total karma in accordance with the order prevailing in the spiritual world*—not in an arbitrary way, but such that the organism of the community becomes an image of the order in the heavens.'[30] In the same lecture, Rudolf Steiner calls this organism 'the foundation of the humanity of the future based on man's ego-nature'.

Only a Society that seeks to work with full consciousness in the field of karma can become a new organ for the activity of the Christ as Lord of Karma in the future. And he needs such organs on the Earth to fulfil his aims for humanity.

We know that after death the human being is initially concerned karmically with himself and with the human beings closely connected with him. He then works with those souls who belonged together with him to the same nation. But when the human being ascends to the Midnight heights, he links himself with all other souls. So that in these spiritual heights we experience a brotherhood encompassing *the whole of humanity*, a brotherhood of human souls all of whom work together on the future of humanity from world karma. This brotherhood can arise in the Midnight Hour only when souls link up together in a way that is possible solely by beholding the karma-forming activity of the First Hierarchy. '[In the Midnight Hour] we experience the fulfilment of our karma in our next Earth life in a supersensible way among the Seraphim, Cherubim and Thrones as a prefiguration of what we will experience as a human being through other human beings ... The gods are truly the creators of the human being, but they also create our karma. Because the gods initially experience our *karmic fulfilments* as a heavenly image, this is impressed upon us as we continue our further existence. We take our karma and its manner of fulfilment upon ourselves because we behold it beforehand in the divine deeds of the Seraphim, Cherubim and Thrones. So in that moment we experience what will happen to us in our next Earth life, carried out by the gods.'[31] Thus, in this most exalted moment of post-mortal existence, human souls receive a powerful *impulse towards brotherhood* together with the cosmic fulfilments of their karma. And the beings of the First Hierarchy want to carry this primal image of brotherhood down into human life. They do this above all through their activity between the ages of 28 and 49 as a significant part of what we have called the karmic fulfilments for this phase of life. This means that behind the ideal of brotherhood lies a power that creates an image of the World Midnight on Earth and thus may be called the World Midday. To realize this will be the greatest future task of the Anthroposophical Society as a community of karma in the making.

How can this be done in concrete terms? The anthroposophical movement began on Earth by the founding of various working groups. Rudolf Steiner visited them and gave lectures. The wisdom teachings of Anthroposophy were studied in these groups. So we may call them study groups. The spiritual work pursued there could lead in the sense of the reverse divine service[32] encountered on the path of modern initiation to crossing the threshold to the spiritual world and could be effective as far as the sphere of the Angels.

Rudolf Steiner then visited several European countries in 1923, and founded the various national societies together with the members of the groups working there in order to create the conditions allowing the fruits of their work to reach the sphere of their respective Folk Archangels.

The representatives of these national societies then founded the General Anthroposophical World Society in Dornach at Christmas 1923 under the direct leadership of Rudolf Steiner. From an esoteric standpoint, the Society was assigned the task of representing modern humanity *vis-à-vis* the Michaelic spirit of the times. After the Christmas Conference, the souls that had already been companions of Michael in their pre-natal existence and formed a great fraternal community in his supersensible school in the Sun-sphere[33] have, as true followers of Michael, the mission of bringing this fraternal community to Earth and realizing it in the form of the General Anthroposophical Society.

This can be achieved when the following is borne in mind. The Angels associated with the work of the study groups can also bring the forces of the entire Third Hierarchy that they represent into this work. In like manner, the Archangels or Folk Spirits acting through the national societies can bring in the forces of the Second Hierarchy, which they represent within the Third Hierarchy. And in the same way the Time Spirit or Arche who guides all of humanity can mediate the highest First Hierarchy whom he represents. Thus Michael can today bring the forces of karmic fulfilment and the associated impulses of brotherhood into the General Anthroposophical Society if its members keep faith with him and with the impulses received in his supersensible school. In this way, the great supersensible community of Michael strives at the present time to do the will of Michael by transforming the forces of the World Midnight into those of the World Midday on the Earth in the form of the General Anthroposophical Society.

And if we feel that the forces of brotherhood are not strong enough in the Society today, then we must honestly admit to ourselves that we have not yet permeated ourselves sufficiently with the will of Michael. This means in particular that we have not entered into relationship with the forces of the First Hierarchy that are working through him, in the period between the ages of 28 and 49.

This shows us the most important task facing us as members of the General Anthroposophical Society. For if we succeed between the ages of 28 and 49 in realizing our karmic fulfilments as the impulse of brotherhood that unites us all, then in the next phase of our lives between our forty-second and sixty-third years we can develop a great creative power in all fields, especially in the social sphere, with the aid of the Second Hierarchy. And this provides the basis for developing the forces for free sacrifice in the following period of life in order to create the new Michaelic karma in the world. In the further course of Earth life, this new karma will then form a seed for the development of what Rudolf Steiner has called the 'Michaelic race' of the future.[34]

Let us finally touch upon another topic, namely, the relation of the karma-forming activity of all three Hierarchies to what Rudolf Steiner called the *world ritual* or *cosmic ritual* in his lecture of 31 December 1922.

In an anthroposophical sense we can speak of two

forms of ritual whose natures are mutually complementary: the sacramental ritual, which is celebrated in the various Churches, including the Christian Community; and what is known as the *reverse ritual*, which is present in anthroposophical groups as a constituent of the modern path of initiation. These two forms of ritual differ in the following way. In the first case spiritual beings descend and are present around the altar in a supersensible manner. In the second case, however, human beings ascend thanks to their conscious efforts in order to dwell among the Angels and still higher hierarchical beings.[35] In other words: in the sacramental ritual in a certain sense the same happens as the human soul experiences when it enters into earthly life through the gate of birth. And what happens in the reverse ritual may be compared with the passage of the soul at the end of life through the gate of death and the subsequent ascent into the spiritual worlds.

In contrast, the cosmic ritual is not linked to earthly conditions. It consists of the joint activities of all three Hierarchies. But the highest activity of these three Hierarchies that the human being may experience takes place in the Midnight Hour between two incarnations. This is where human karma is formed in association with the entire cosmos under the guidance of the First Hierarchy. Rudolf Steiner affirms that this is 'something far more stupendous' than the entire 'splendour of the heavenly firmament'.[36] The karma-forming activity then revealed from the beyond in the highest spiritual world appears from Earth as the visible cosmos of stars and planets. In this connection, Rudolf Steiner once posed the question as to why the Hierarchies had created the cosmos, and answered: in order to bring karma into manifestation.

Understood in this way, the cosmos is transformed into a great temple in which the human being increasingly becomes a being capable of free sacrifice. For, after he has fulfilled his old karma, he can add something new to the existing cosmos from out of himself, from his free ego. 'The world becomes a temple, the world becomes the house of God. The knowing human being, rising to activity in feeling and willing, becomes capable of sacrifice. The basic relation between the human being and the world ascends from that of knowledge to world ritual, to cosmic ritual.'[37] And if the human being can allow the Midnight forces to flow into his social activities on Earth as Midday forces in the way described above, then Earth life itself is transformed into an image of this cosmic ritual. This combines the two other forms of ritual, the sacramental and reverse ones, which in turn are linked to unbornness and immortality, and allows them to partake of eternity. In this way, a true knowledge of karma leads to a completely new relationship with the world. Rudolf Steiner expresses this in the following way: 'Everything that makes up our relationship to the world must initially become aware of itself as a cosmic ritual in the human being. That is the first beginning of what must happen if Anthroposophy is to carry out its mission in the world.'

What humanity received merely as a 'first beginning' of this cosmic ritual through Anthroposophy in 1922 was transformed at the Christmas Conference into a basis upon which man can participate in this cosmic ritual.

This basis forms the foundation stone of the Christmas Conference: the 'dodecahedral stone of love'[38] of the new community, which can gradually become 'an image of the heavenly order' by virtue of our relationship to the beings of the Third Hierarchy described above.[39]

This represents the most important task that Rudolf Steiner entrusted to his pupils through his research into karma. It must be fulfilled to a certain degree before the end of the century. For the culmination of the anthroposophical movement forecast by Rudolf Steiner depends on this fulfilment.

That is what Michael expects from the General Anthroposophical Society today.

Notes

RSP = Rudolf Steiner Press, London
AP = Anthroposophic Press, New York
GA = *Gesamtausgabe*. Reference is to the volume number from the catalogue of the collected edition of Rudolf Steiner's works in the original German (published by Rudolf Steiner Verlag, Dornach, Switzerland).

1 See the end of Book X.
2 See also: Prokofieff, S.O., *Rudolf Steiner and the Founding of the New Mysteries*, 2nd ed., Temple Lodge Publishing 1994, Chapter 4.
3 See Steiner, R., *Karmic Relationships*, Vol. 2 (GA 236), RSP 1974, lecture of 18 May 1924, and Vol. 5 (GA 239), RSP 1984, lecture of 8 June 1924.
4 Steiner, R., *A Road to Self Knowledge* (GA 16), RSP 1975, lecture of 10 January 1915.
5 Steiner, R., *The Four Mystery Plays* (GA 14), RSP 1982, 'The Guardian of the Threshold', Scene 6.
6 See also Marie Steiner's foreword to the first edition of the shorthand record of the Christmas Conference, in: Steiner, R., *The Christmas Conference for the Foundation of the General Anthroposophical Society 1923–1924* (GA 260), RSP/AP 1990, and Ita Wegman's essay of 7 June 1925 in: Wegman, I., *Esoteric Studies. The Michael Impulse*, Temple

Lodge Publishing 1993, as well as: Prokofieff, S.O., *Rudolf Steiner and the Founding of the New Mysteries*, 2nd ed., Temple Lodge Publishing 1994, Chapter 3.
7 See the lectures by Rudolf Steiner in GA 333, *Karmic Relationships*, Vol. 3 (GA 237), RSP 1977, Vol. 4 (GA 238), RSP 1983, Vol. 6 (GA 240), RSP 1989, and Vol. 8 (GA 240), RSP 1975.
8 See Steiner, R., *From Jesus to Christ* (GA 131), RSP 1991, lecture of 14 October 1911, and *Esoteric Christianity and the Mission of Christian Rosenkreutz* (GA 130), RSP 1984, lecture of 2 December 1911.
9 Steiner, R., *The Gospel of St Matthew* (GA 123), RSP 1965, lecture of 11 September 1910.
10 Steiner, R., *The Four Mystery Plays* (op. cit.), 'The Guardian of the Threshold', Scene 8.
11 Steiner, R., *The Spiritual Guidance of the Individual and Humanity* (GA 15), AP 1992, Chapter 3.
12 Steiner, R., *Karmic Relationships*, Vol. 2 (GA 236) (op. cit.).
13 See Steiner, R., *Philosophy, Cosmology and Religion* (GA 215), AP 1984, lecture of 15 September 1922.
14 See Steiner, R., *From Symptom to Reality in Modern History* (GA 185), RSP 1976, lecture of 2 November 1918.
15 Steiner, R., *Karmic Relationships*, Vol. 2 (GA 236) (op. cit.), lecture of 18 May 1924.
16 Ibid., lecture of 29 May 1924.
17 Verse written by Rudolf Steiner for Marie Steiner, Christmas 1922 (in GA 40).
18 Steiner, R., *The Spiritual Hierarchies and their Reflection in the Physical World* (GA 110), AP 1983, lecture of 15 April 1909, evening.
19 As Note 17.
20 As Note 12.

21 Rudolf Steiner referred to this supersensible stream of time as having an 'occult-astral' character in the 'Manuscript of Barr', in: Steiner R./Marie Steiner-von Sivers, *Correspondence and Documents 1901–1925* (GA 262), RSP/AP 1988.
22 In: Steiner, R., *Spiritual Relations in the Human Organism* (GA 218). Mercury Press, New York 1984.
23 As Note 14.
24 See Steiner, R., *Karmic Relationships*, Vol. 3 (GA 237) (op. cit.), lectures of 3 and 8 August 1924.
25 For references to the School of Michael and the supersensible ritual, see the lectures of Rudolf Steiner in *Karmic Relationships* Vol. 3 (GA 237) (op. cit.), Vol. 4 (GA 238) (op. cit.), and Vol. 6 (GA 240) (op. cit.).
26 See Steiner, R., *Karmic Relationships*, Vol. 3 (GA 237) (op. cit.), lecture of 8 August 1924.
27 Rudolf Steiner spoke subsequently in several lectures about this risk and the affirmation of his deed by higher powers, e.g. on 23 May, 18 July and 24 August 1924.
28 In: Steiner, R., *How can Mankind Find the Christ Again?* (GA 187) AP 1984.
29 See Steiner, R., *The Spiritual Hierarchies and their Reflection in the Spiritual World* (GA 110) (op. cit.), lecture of 18 April 1909, evening.
30 See Note 9.
31 Steiner, R., *Karmic Relationships* (GA 238), Vol. 5, RSP 1984.
32 Steiner, R., *Awakening to Community* (GA 257), AP 1974, lectures of 27 February and 3 March 1923.
33 See Note 26.
34 See Steiner, R., *Karmic Relationships*, Vol. 3, (op. cit.) lecture of 3 August 1924.
35 See Steiner, R., *Awakening to Community* (GA 257) (op.

cit.), lecture of 3 March 1923.
36 Steiner, R., *Karmic Relationships*, Vol. 5 (GA 239) (op. cit.), lecture of 31 March 1924.
37 Steiner, R., *Man and the World of the Stars* (GA 219), AP 1963, lecture of 31 December 1922 as well as the following quotation.
38 Steiner, R., *The Christmas Conference for the Foundation of the General Anthroposophical Society 1923–1924* (GA 260) (op. cit.), lecture of 25 December 1923.
39 As Note 31.